piano • guitar • vocal

indigo girls

rites of passage

CONTENTS

MANAGEMENT: Russell Carter Artist Management, Ltd.

Cover Photo by: Michael Lavine
Cover Artwork by: Karen Chance

ISBN 0-7935-1722-2

Hal Leonard Publishing Corporation
7777 West Bluemound Road P.O. Box 13819 Milwaukee, WI 53213

 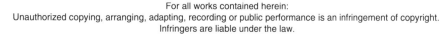

biography

On *RITES OF PASSAGE*, the fifth release on Epic by the Indigo Girls, a song called "Jonas & Ezekiel" begins with a few seconds of eerie ambient sound.

"That's Cooper Seay of the Ellen James Society, playing a backwards guitar track, "explains the Indigos' Amy Ray, "and me, taking my watch off and putting it on the music stand before I started singing. They're almost accidental sounds, and that's the kind of thing that makes this album something different for us. I've always wanted to do stuff like that on a record, but we never had time to experiment in the studio that way before."

Rights of Passage really *is* "something different" for the Indigo Girls. There's a sense of adventure in the eclectic instrumentation, and a rolling rhythmic undercurrent created as much by Latin and African percussion as by a standard trap set. There's a new sense of maturity in the songwriting of Emily Saliers and Amy Ray, and a renewed sense of vitality – of *bite*, if you will – in their delivery.

Unlike past Indigos albums, many of these twelve original songs were never performed live prior to their recording. That, say Emily Saliers, "is the freshness of this album, that we cut these songs without any preconceived notions of how they should sound."

Rites of Passage was produced by Peter Collins, whose name is sure to raise eyebrows among those familiar with his best-selling hard-rock records with the likes of Qeensryche and Alice Cooper. "Amy and I had talked to other producers, but Peter's name kept coming up from people we respected," explains Emily. "We thought 'No way we'll wanna work with this guy!'"

"But when we met in Atlanta, Peter said all the right things. He was interested in using more exotic instruments – the Eastern percussion, the Irish fiddle – and didn't have any ego thing going on. A perfect combination of professionalism and the willingness to try far-out things." Collins, she adds, "could produce any kind of music."

Photo by: Laura Levine

Rites of Passage was recorded by Pat McCarthy (U2, Waterboys) at Bearsville Studios in Woodstock, New York and mixed by David Leonard in Los Angeles. With Amy and Emily on guitars and vocals, the supporting cast includes bassist Sara Lee (of B-52's fame) and drummers Jerry Marotta, Kenny Aronoff and Budgie of Siouxie & the Banshees.

Special guests include violinist Lisa Germano (of the John Mellencamp band), guitarist John Jennings (from Mary-Chapin Carpenter's group), and another Banshee, Martin McCarrick, on cello. The Indigos "have been Roches fans since we were kids," says Emily, and having the three sisters join in on "Airplane" and "Virginia Woolf" was "a major treat – the same goes for Jackson Browne and David Crosby (harmony vocals on "Galileo" and "Let It Be Me"). Grammy-winning composer and arranger Michael Kamen arranged the strings for "Ghost". Atlanta musicians Cooper Seay and Michael Lorant of Big Fish Ensemble also contributed musical parts.

Fan Club information: write c/o
Russell Carter Artist Management, Ltd.
315 W. Ponce De Leon Avenue, Suite 755
Decatur, GA 30030

discography

1985

Indigo Girls make their recording debut in the summer with the single, "Crazy Game" b/w "Someone To Come Home," issued on their own Indigo label.

1986

An EP, *Indigo Girls*, produced and engineered by Frank French and Kristen Hall, is released on their own Indigo label in November. Songs include "Cold As Ice", "Finlandia", "History Of Us", "Land Of Canaan", "Lifeblood", and "Never Stop".

1987

Strange Fire, Indigo Girls' first full-length album, is released on Indigo Records in the fall. This limited-edition disc, produced by Amy, Emily and John Keane, includes the original versions of "Blood And Fire" and "Land Of Canaan" plus "Left Me A Fool", "StrangeFire", "Crazy Game" and six more.

1988

Indigo Girls sign with Epic Records. Their self-titled label debut album is recorded in Los Angeles with producer Scott Litt in the fall. Participating musicians include Peter Buck, Mike Mills and Bill Berry of R.E.M. ("Tried To Be True"). Michael Stipe of R.E.M. ("Kid Fears"), Hothouse Flowers ("Closer To Fine", "Secure Yourself"), and Luka Bloom ("Closer To Fine").

1989

Indigo Girls is released in February. A single, "Closer To Fine", enters the *Billboard* Top 100 in July and reaches #52; the album peaks at #22 and remains on the chart for 35 weeks. Indigo Girls tour as club headliners and as support to R.E.M. and Neil Young. *Indigo Girls* is certified gold in September, and *Strange Fire* is reissued on Epic in November with an added bonus track, the Youngbloods' "Get Together". A "Get Together" video is created in cooperation with the non-profit housing group, Habitat For Humanity. In the 32nd Annual Grammy Awards, the Indigos are nominated for "Best New Artist" and *Indigo Girls* is voted "Best Contemporary Folk Recording".

1990

In January Indigo Girls' first home video, *Live At The Uptown Lounge*, is released by Sony Music Video. In May Indigo Girls headline a benefit concert for the Children's Health Fund at the personal invitation of CHF founder Paul Simon. A new Epic album, *Nomads*Indians*Saints*, produced by Scott Litt, is recorded in Athens, Georgia and Los Angeles in the summer and released in September. The supporting cast includes drummers Kenny Aronoff and Jim Keltner, bassist Sara Lee, Mary-Chapin Carpenter (backing vocals on "Hammer And A Nail" and "Southland In The Springtime"), and Daemon Records recording artists The Ellen James Society ("1-2-3"). Indigo Girls' single, "A Hammer And A Nail", is nominated for a Grammy Award as "Best Contemporary Folk Recording".

1991

In January Indigo Girls make their first appearance on the *Tonight Show* with Jay Leno. In June Epic releases an eight-song live EP, *Back On The Bus Y'All*, recorded at Notre Dame University, West Georgia College, and the Uptown Lounge in Athens, Georgia, plus "1-2-3" from Nomads*Indians*Saints. In December Indigo Girls make their fourth appearance on Late Night With David Letterman. In the 34th Annual Grammy Awards *Back On The Bus Y'All* is nominated for "Best Contemporary Folk Album" – Indigo Girls' fourth Grammy nomination.

1992

Rites of Passage, Indigo Girls' fifth Epic release, is issued in May.

airplane

Up on the airplane nearer my God to thee
I start making a deal inspired by gravity

If I did wrong I won't do it again
I can be good and sweet and nice
And if I had some enemies they're friends
I hold on to my life with the grip of vice

Up on the airplane nearer my God to thee
I start making a deal inspired by gravity

That little spot on the ground is my hometown
I like to call it my home and it's sweet
I'd rather take a seat down there
Than a throne up here
Up above 30,000 feet
And I'm up on the airplane
I never should've read my horoscope
Or the fortune on the bubble gum strip
Saying what you don't think will happen will
Great thing to read before a trip on an airplane

Pilot says the big blue sky's like a swimming pool
Big fluffy clouds like a feather bed
I'd rather have a real pillow underneath my head
Lying in my bed which is in my hometown
Which is on the ground far from an airplane
Far from an airplane up on the airplane
Up on the (I'll be making a deal)
Up on the (I'll be making a deal)
Up on the (I'll be making a deal)

Words and Music by Emily Saliers

airplane

Words and Music by
EMILY SALIERS

Up on the air - plane, _____ near - er, my God, _ to thee, _

I start mak - ing a deal _____ in -

spir - ed by grav - i - ty. _ If I did wrong_ I won't do _ it a - gain_

That lit - tle spot _ on the ground_ is my _

_ blue_ sky's _ like a swim-

Guitarists: play alternate voicing (see Guitar section)

cedar tree

You dug a well
You dug it deep
For every wife you buried
You planted a cedar tree
The best you ever had

I stand where you stood
I stand for bad or good
I am green
You are wood
The best he ever had

I dig a well
I dig it deep
And for only my love
I plant a cedar tree
The best we ever had

Words and Music by Amy Ray

cedar tree

Words and Music by
AMY RAY

*Vocal is written 8va higher than sung.

Instrumental solo

*Guitarists: play alternate voicing (see Guitar section)

chickenman

I am an only child born of the wild
Riddled to spend my time defending my land
You are my only one born in the sun
Riddled to spend your time defending my plan
Dead dog on the highway
Median cats are growling at me
I turn my lights on brighter
Counting through the nightride

One more life for the taker
Chickenman
One more song for the maker
Chickenman

On the road to Athens
I saw a dead deer on the highway
I slipped into a desert
Five prairie dogs and a rabbit
I was running down on Queen Street
I saw a woman on the sidewalk
She was beaten by a stranger
Danger Danger Danger

One more life for the taker
Chickenman Chickenman Chickenman hold my hand
One more life for the maker
Hold my hand Chickenman

I was on the road to Austin
I met a man on the highway

He sold me junk and conversation
He was wise and dirty from the weather
I said darkness into darkness
All the carnage of my journeys
Makes it hard to be living
He said it's a long road to be forgiven

One more life for the taker
Chickenman Chickenman Chickenman hold my hand
One more song for the maker
Chickenman Chickenman Chickenman hold my hand

I am an only child born of the wild
Riddled to spend my time defending my land
You are my only one born in the the sun
Riddled to spend your time defending my plan

I went looking for a car
Found myself beneath the stars
I went looking for a girl
Found a man and his world

Chickenman Chickenman Chickenman hold my hand
I am an only child hold my hand
Chickenman Chickenman Chickenman hold my hand

Words and Music by Amy Ray

chickenman

Words and Music by
AMY RAY

Vocal is written 8va higher than sung.

Moderately, lively

Dead dog — on the high - way, —

me - di - an cats are growl - ing at me. I turn my lights on bright -

er. _____ I'm count - ing through _ the night _ ride _____

I went look - ing for a car,__ found my-self__ be - neath__ the stars.

I went look - ing for a girl,__ found a man__ and __ his world.

Repeat ad lib.

Chick - en - man,__ Chick - en - man,__ Chick - en - man,__ hold __ my hand.

D/F♯   D5

Chick-en - man,__ Chick-en-man,__ Chick-en - man,__ hold__ my hand.__

rit.

galileo

Galileo's head was on the block
The crime was looking up the truth
As the bombshells of my daily fears explode
I try to trace them to my youth
Then you had to bring up reincarnation
Over a couple of beers the other night
Now I'm serving time for mistakes
Made by another in another lifetime

How long till my soul gets it right
Can any human being ever reach that kind of light
I call on the resting soul of Galileo
King of night vision king of insight

I think about my fear of motion
Which I never could explain
Some other fool across the ocean years ago
Must have crashed his little airplane

How long till my soul gets it right
Can any human being ever reach that kind of light
I call on the resting soul of Galileo
King of night vision king of insight

I'm not making a joke
You know me I take everything so seriously

If we wait for the time till all souls get it right
Then at least I know there'll be no
Nuclear annihilation in my lifetime
I'm still not right

I offer thanks to those before me
That's all I've got to say
Maybe you squandered big bucks in your lifetime
Now I've got to pay
But then again it feels like some sort of inspiration
To let the next life off the hook
Or she'll say look what I had to overcome
From my last life
I think I'll write a book

How long till my soul gets it right
Can any human being ever reach that kind of light
I call on the resting soul of Galileo
King of night vision king of insight

How long, how long, how long

Words and Music by Emily Saliers

galileo

Words and Music by
EMILY SALIERS

30

ghost

There's a letter on the desktop that I dug out of a drawer
The last truce we ever came to from our adolescent war
And I start to feel a fever from the warm air through the screen
You come regular like seasons shadowing my dreams

And the Mississippi's mighty but it starts in Minnesota
At a place where you could walk across with five steps down
And I guess that's how you started like a pinprick to my heart
But at this point you rush right through me and I start to drown

And there's not enough room in this world for my pain
Signals cross and love gets lost and time passed makes it plain
Of all my demon spirits I need you the most
I'm in love with your ghost I'm in love with your ghost

Dark and dangerous like a secret that gets whispered in a hush
(Don't tell a soul)
When I wake the things I dreamt about you last night make me blush
(Don't tell a soul)
When you kiss me like a lover then you sting me like a viper
I go follow to the river play your memory like the piper

And I feel it like a sickness how this love is killing me
But I'd walk into the fingers of your fire willingly
And dance the edge of sanity I've never been this close
In love with your ghost

Ooooh . . .

Unknowing captor you'll never know how much you
Pierce my spirit but I can't touch you
Can you hear it a cry to be free
Or I'm forever under lock and key as you pass through me

Now I see your face before me
        I would launch a thousand ships
To bring your heart back to my island
        As the sand beneath me slips

As I burn up in your presence and I know now how it feels
To be weakened by Achilles with you always at my heels
And my bitter pill to swallow is the the silence that I keep
That poisons me I can't swim free the river is too deep
Though I'm baptized by your touch I am no worse at most
In love with your ghost

Words and Music by Emily Saliers

ghost

Words and Music by
EMILY SALIERS

34

*Guitarists: play alternate voicing (see Guitar section)

jonas & ezekial

I left my anger in a river running Highway Five
New Hampshire Vermont Border by
college farms hubcaps and falling rocks
voices in the woods and the mountain tops
I used to search for reservations and native lands
before I realized everywhere stand
There have been tribal feet running wild as fire
Some past life sister of my desire

Jonas and Ezekial hear me now
Steady now don't come out
I'm not ready for the dead to show its face
Whose turn is it anyway?

When I was young my people taught me well
Give back what you take or you'll go to Hell
It's not the devil's land you know it's not that kind
Every devil I meet becomes a friend of mine
Every devil I meet is an angel in disguise

Jonas and Ezekial hear me now
Steady now don't come out
I'm not ready for the dead to show its face
Whose turn is it anyway?

White chain rope fear be still my dear
A bullet in the head now he's dead
A friend of a friend someone said
He was an activist with a very short life
I think there's a lesson here he died without a fight
In the war over land where the world began
Prophecy says it's where the world will end
But there's a tremor growing in our own backyard
Fear in our heads fear in our hears prophets in the graveyard

Jonas and Ezekial hear me now
Steady now don't come out
I'm not ready for the dead to show its face
Whose turn is it anyway?

Jonas and Ezekial hear me now
Steady now I feel your ghost about
I'm not ready for the dead to show its face
Whose angel are you anyway?

Words and Music by Amy Ray

jonas & ezekial

Words and Music by
AMY RAY

42

46

let it be me

Sticks and stones battle zones
A single lightbulb on a single thread for the black
Sirens wail history fails
Rose-colored glass begins to age and crack
While the politicians shadow box the power ring
In an endless split decision never solve anything
From a neighbor's distant land
I heard the strain of the common man

Let it be me (this is not a fighting song)
Let it be me (not a wrong for a wrong)
Let it be me, if the world is night
Shine my life like a light

Well the world seems spent and the President
Has no good idea of who the masses are
Well I'm one of them and I'm among friends
Trying to see beyond the fences of our own backyard
I've seen kingdoms blow like ashes
                        in the winds of change
But the power of truth
                        is the fuel for the flame
So the darker the ages get
                        there's a stronger beacon yet

Let it be me (this is not a fighting song)
Let it be me (not a wrong for a wrong)
Let it be me, if the world is night
Shine my life like a light

In the kind word you speak in the turn of the cheek
When your vision stays clear in the face of your fear
then you see turning off a lightswitch
                        is their only power
When we stand like spotlights in a mighty tower
All for one and one for all
Then we sing the common call

Let it be me (this is not a fighting song)
Let it be me (not a wrong for a wrong)
Let it be me, if the world is night
Shine my life like a light

Words and Music by Emily Saliers

let it be me

49

Words and Music by
EMILY SALIERS

Sticks and stones,__ bat - tle zones.__ A sin - gle light bulb on a sin - gle
world seems spent __ and the pres - i - dent __ has no good i - de - a of who the

thread for the black.__ Si - rens __ wail, ____ his -t'ry fails.__
mass - es are. Well, I'm one of them and I'm a - mong friends._ We're try'n to

* Guitarists: play alternate voicing (see guitar section)

love will come to you

Guess I wasn't the best one to ask
Me myself with my face pressed up against love's glass
To see the shiny toy I've been hoping for
The one I never can afford

The wide world spins and spits turmoil
And the nations toil for peace
But the paws of fear upon your chest
Only love can soothe that beast

And my words are paper tigers
No match for the predator of pain inside her

I say love will come to you
Hoping just because I spoke the words that they're true
As if I've offered up a crystal ball to look through
Where there's now one there will be two

I was born under the sign of Cancer
Like brushing cloth I smooth the wrinkles for an answer

I close my eyes and wish you fine
(I'm always closing my eyes wishing I'm fine)
Even though I know your not this time
(Even though I'm not this time)

I say love will come to you
Hoping just because I spoke the words that they're true
As if I've offered up a crystal ball to look through
Where there's now one there will be two

Dodging your memories a field of knives
Always on the outside looking in on other's lives

I say love will come to you
Hoping just because I spoke the words that they're true
As if I've offered up a crystal ball to look through
Where there's now one there will be two

And I wish her insight to the battle of love's blindness
Strength from the milk of human kindness
A safe place for all the pieces that scattered
Learn to pretend there's more to love that matters

Words and Music by Emily Saliers

love will come to you

Words and Music by
EMILY SALIERS

Guitarists: play alternate voicing (see guitar section)

the piec - es that scat - tered, learn to pre - tend

there's more than love that mat - ters.

Vocal 1st time only

nashville

As I drive from your pearly gates
I realize that I just can't stay
All those mountains they keep you locked inside
And hid the truth from my slighted eyes
I came to you with a half open heart
Dreams upon my back
Illusions of a brand new start

Nashville can't I carry the load
Is it my fault I can't reap what I sow?
Nashville did you give me half a chance
With your southern style and your hidden dance?

All those voices they whisper through my walls
They talk of falling fast
They say I'm losing it all
They say I'm running blind to a love of my own
But I'll be walking proud
I'm saving what I still own

I fell on my knees to kiss your land
But you are so far down I can't even see to stand

Nashville you forgot the human race
You see with half a mind what colors hide the face
Nashville I'd like to know your fate
I'd like to stay awhile but I've seen your lowered state today

I'm leaving but I've got all these debts to pay
We all have our dues I'll pay in some other place
I never ask that you pay me back
We all arrive with more I left with less than I had

Your town is made for people passing through
A last chance for a cause well I thought I knew

Nashville tell me what you gonna do
With your southern style it'll never pull you through
Nashville I can't place no blame
But if you forget my face I'll never call your name again

I fell on my knees to kiss your land
But you are so far down can't even see to stand

Nashville you forgot the human race
You see with half a mind what colors hide the face
Nashville I'd like to know your fate
I'd like to stay awhile but I've seen your lowered state today
I'm running away

Words and Music by Amy Ray

nashville

Words and Music by
AMY RAY

Moderately, not too fast

Capo 2nd Fret
Guitar: A
Keyboard: B

As I drive_____ from your_ es _ they whis-per

_ pearl-y gates_ I_ re-a-lize_ that I
through my walls._ They talk of fall-ing fast. They say I'm
_ debts to pay. You know we all have our dues._____ I'll pay in

just can't stay._ All those moun-tains, they kept you
los-ing it all. They say I'm run-ning blind to a
some oth-er place._ I never ask that you

64

66

joking

You said the world was magic
I was wide-eyed and laughing
We were dancing up to the bright side
Forget about your ego forget about your pride
And you will never have to compromise

But you were only joking

We talked about our mothers
Kissed the wounds of our fathers
I could've been your sister
I would've been your brother
You kissed me like I was a soldier heading for war
I'm a dying man but I don't know what for

But you were only joking
You were only joking brother

Gravel and glass on the bottom of my feet
I bruised my heels on the swollen street
We were girls in bars
We were boys on the town
Bumping like a pinball off a careless crowd
You said good friends are hard to come by
I laughed and bought you a beer
'Cause it's too corny to cry
Well sentiment given and sentiment lost
You shook it off with a smirk and a toss

And you were only joking
You were only joking brother

Words and Music by Amy Ray

joking

Words and Music by
AMY RAY

Fast, with intensity

You said the world was mag - ic. I was wide -
talked a-bout__ moth - ers, kissed the wounds__
said good friends are hard to come__

- eyed and laugh - ing. We were danc - ing up
__ of our fa - thers. I could've been your sis - ter, I
__ by. I laughed and bought you a beer 'cause it's

to the bright__ side. For - get a - bout__ your e - go, for -
would've been your broth - er. You kissed me like I was__ a sol - dier
too corn - y to__ cry. Well, sen - ti - ment__ giv - en and

70

three hits

Three hits to the heart son
And it's poetry in motion
One could send you down the river
Three's a strange way to be delivered

Would you trade your words for freedom
That's a barter for a blind man
Three hits to the heart son
Poetry in motion

Are you levee'd like a treasure
Only words can help me find you
And this world's a frickle measure
I would painfully remind you

From a wise man to a red hand
You lay covered in our best sins
Three hits to the heart son
Poetry in motion

Well I dream you constant stranger
With your best bloods and your anger
You say mother would you claim me
My beloved do you blame me

Well the first two might release you
But the last one sings in me son
Three hits to the heart son
Poetry in motion

* dedicated to the memory of a great poet: Frank Stanford.

Words and Music by Amy Ray

three hits

Words and Music by
AMY RAY

* Vocal written 8va higher than sung.

76

virginia woolf

Some will strut and some will fret
See this an hour on the stage
Others will not but they'll sweat
In their hopelessness in their rage
We're all the same
The men of anger and the women of the page

They published your diary that's how I got to know
you
Key to the room of your own and a mind without end
Here's a young girl on a kind of a telephone line
through time
The voice at the other end comes like a long lost
friend

So I know I'm alright my life will come my life will go
Still I feel it's alright I just got a letter to my soul
When my whole life is on the tip of my tongue
Empty pages for the no longer young
The apathy of time laughs in my face
You say each life has its place

The hatches were battened thunderclouds rolled and
the critics stormed
Battles surrounded the white flag of your youth
But if you need to know that you weathered the
storm of cruel mortality
A hundred years later I'm sitting here living proof

So you know it's alright your life will come your life
will go

Still you'll feel it's alright someone will get a letter to
your soul
When your whole life was on the tip of your tongue
Empty pages for the no longer young
The apathy of time laughed in your face did you hear
me say
Each life has its place

The place where you hold me is dark in a pocket of
truth
The moon has swallowed the sun and the light of the
earth
And so it was for you when the river eclipsed your life
But sent your soul like a message in a bottle to me
And it was my rebirth

So we know it's alright life will come and life will go
Still we know it's alright someone will get a message
to your soul
Then you know it's alright and you feel it's alright
(when my whole life is on the tip of my tongue empty
pages for the no longer young)
Then you know it's alright and you feel it's alright
(each life has its place you say each life has its place)
It's alright

Words and Music by Emily Saliers

virginia woolf

Words and Music by
EMILY SALIERS

Some will ____ strut and ___ some will ____ fret, see this ___ an hour ___ on ___ the stage. ___

Guitarists: play alternate voicing (see guitar section)

84

Photo by: Michael Lavine

Photo by: Susan Alzner   NY 6-4-92

Photo by: Susan Alzner   NY 6-4-92

Photo by: Brannin L. Tanaka   Jerry Marotta on drums

Photo by: Brannin L. Tanaka

Photo by: Susan Alzner '92

Photo by: Cooper Seay   Jane Scarpantoni (cello), Budgie (drums) and Amy in Amsterdam '92

Photo by: D.J. Freed Video shoot for Joking 7-92

Photo by: Susan Alzner 10-2-92

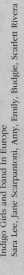

Indigo Girls and band In Europe
Sara Lee, Jane Scarpantoni, Amy, Emily, Budgie, Scarlett Rivera

Photo by: Susan Alzner   NY 6-4-92

Photo by: Susan Alzner   Jerry Marotta on drums Central Park '92

Photo by: Amy
Martin Tillman (cello) on tour with
Indigo Girls '92

Photo by: Susan Alzner   Scarlett Rivera Central Park '92

Photo by: Susan Alzner   Sara Lee

guitar section

Photo by: Laura Levine

The Indigo girls are not only gifted singers and songwriters, they are interesting and exciting guitarists as well. To help you understand the way they use guitars, we have included this special guitar section, which gives you all of their chord voicings, intros, solos and strum patterns in both standard notation and tablature. When a song makes use of a non-standard tuning or a capo, you will find the necessary information at the beginning of the song. Have fun.

Michael P. Wolfsohn
Guitar Editor

cedar tree
(Guitar Parts)

Words and Music by
AMY RAY

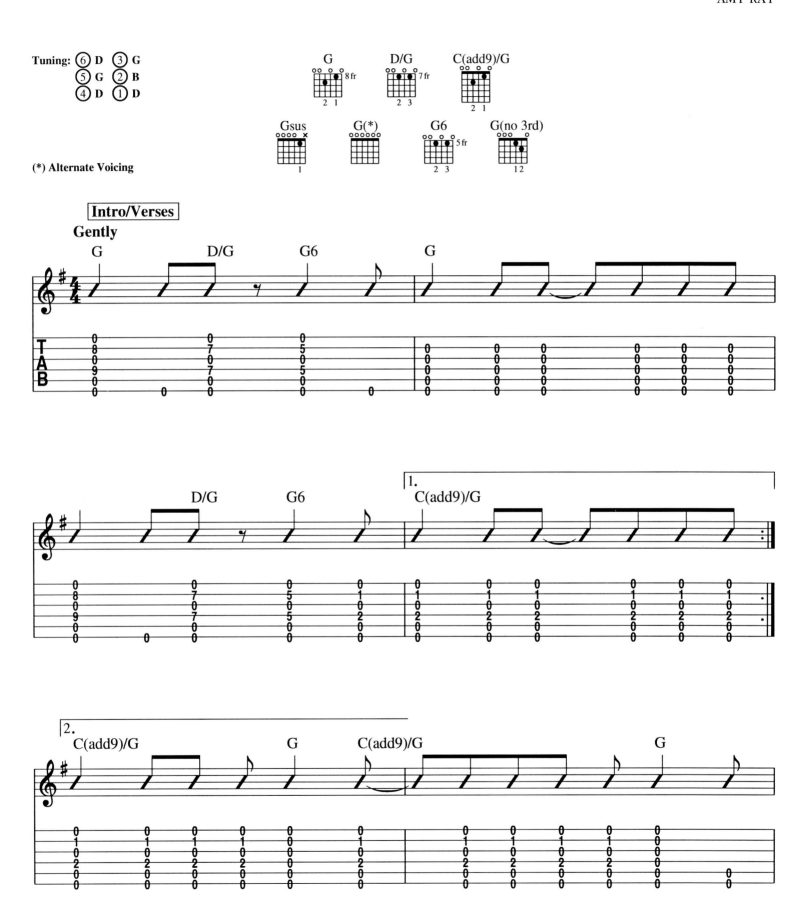

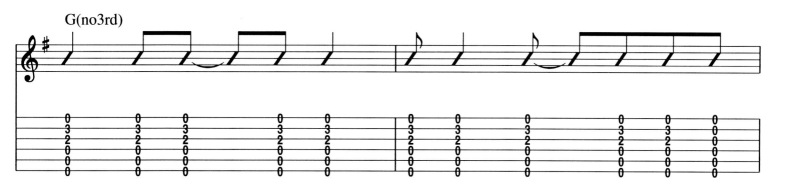

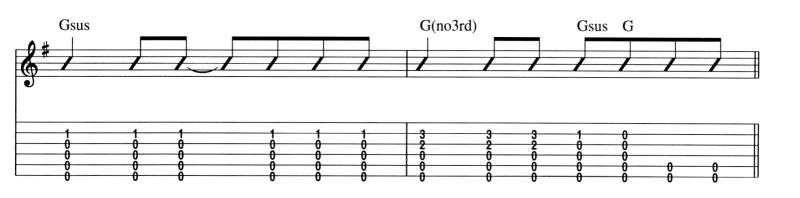

Fill 1 - *Play between verses 1 & 2*

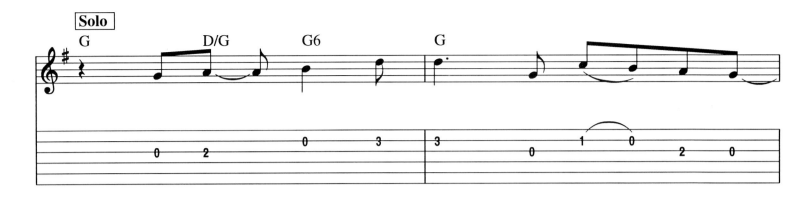

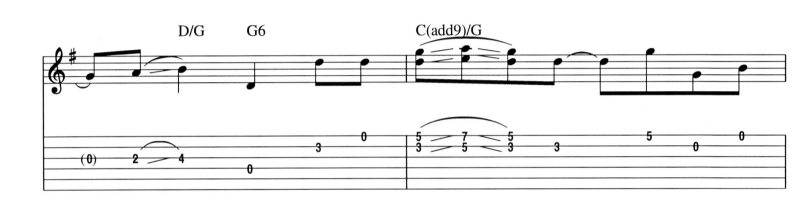

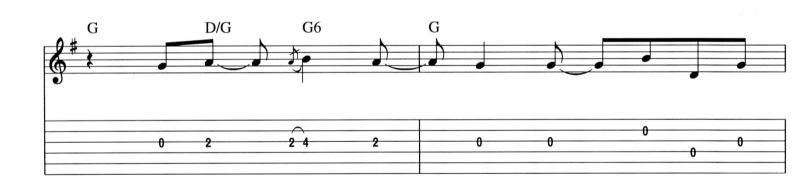

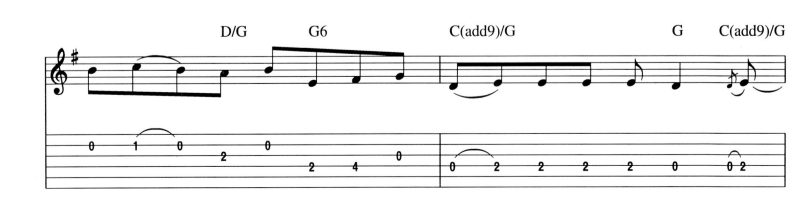

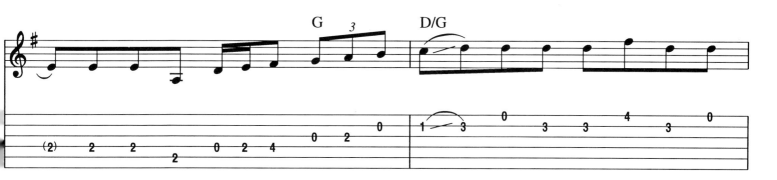

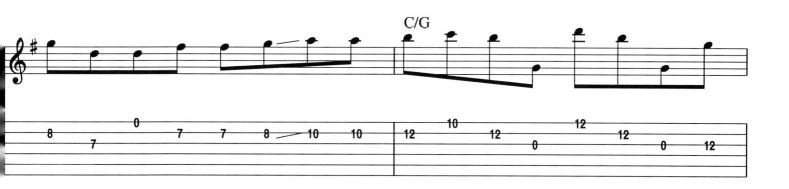

Hoe down is played with a slide guitar as rhythm. Barring D on 7th fret to open G, then C on 5th fret to open G.

chickenman
(Guitar Parts)

Words and Music by
AMY RAY

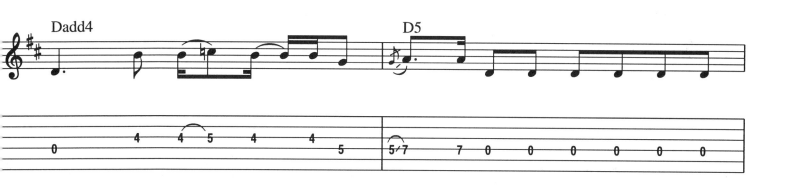

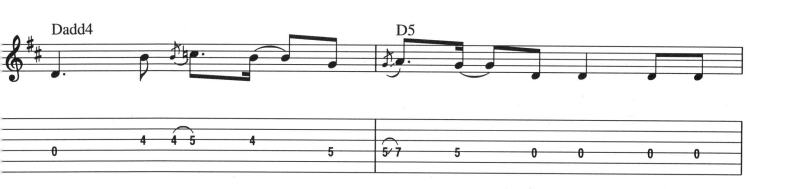

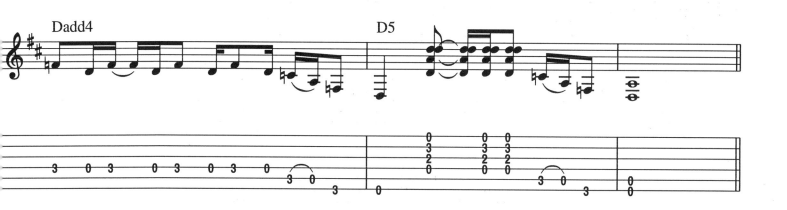

galileo
(Guitar Parts)

Words and Music by
EMILY SALIERS

Tuning: ⑥ D ③ G
⑤ A ② B
④ D ① C

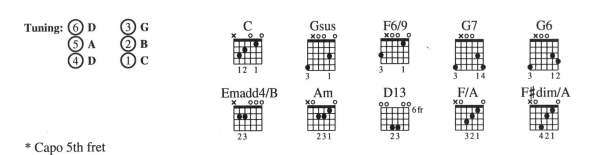

C   Gsus   F6/9   G7   G6

Emadd4/B   Am   D13   F/A   F#dim/A

* Capo 5th fret

Intro

With motion

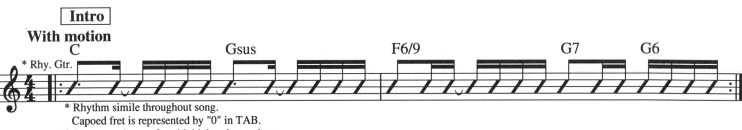

* Rhy. Gtr.

* Rhythm simile throughout song.
  Capoed fret is represented by "0" in TAB.
* Song sounds a perfect 4th higher than written.

Intro

Acoustic Lead 1

Acoustic Lead 2

Acoustic Guitar Solo

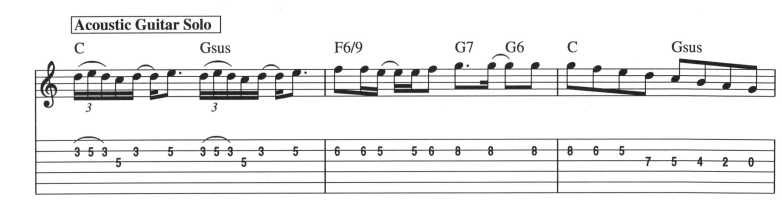

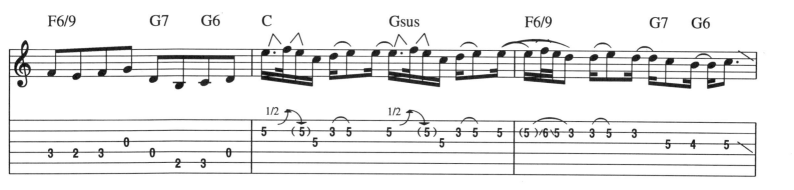

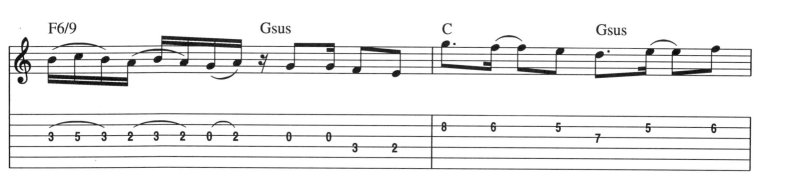

Words and Music by
EMILY SALIERS

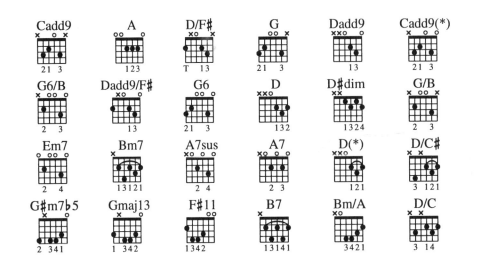

* Alternate Voicing

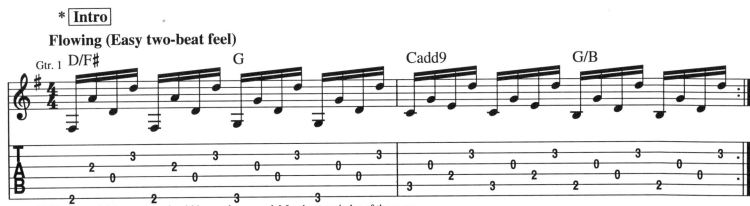

* This fingerpicking pattern should be used as a model for the remainder of the song.

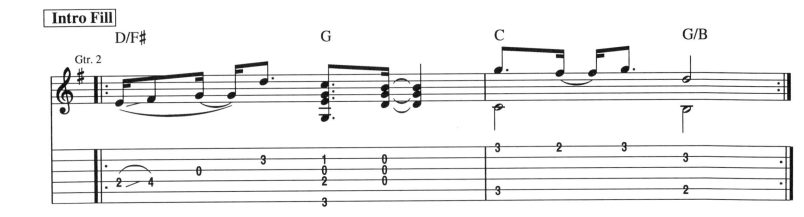

End of Verse

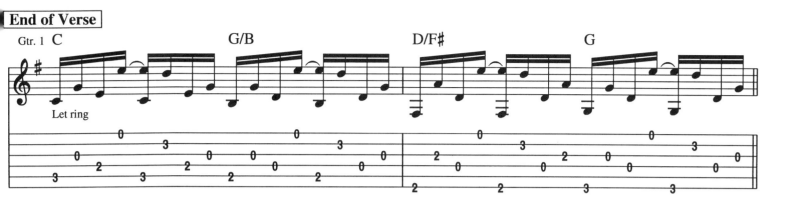

Strumming Pattern 1

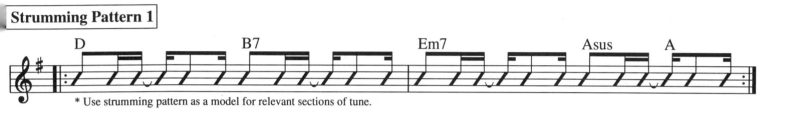

* Use strumming pattern as a model for relevant sections of tune.

Strumming Pattern 2

joking
(Guitar Parts)

Words and Music by
AMY RAY

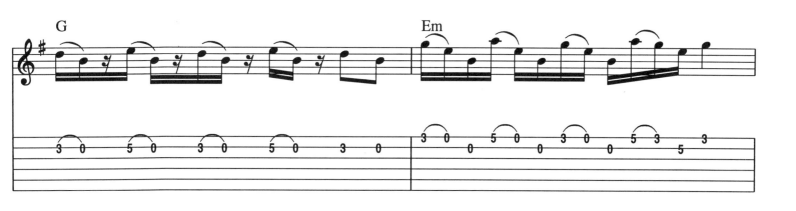

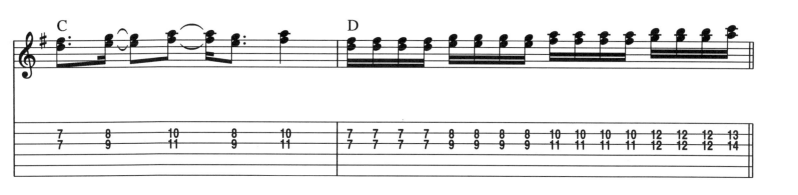

airplane
(Guitar Parts)

Words and Music by
EMILY SALIERS

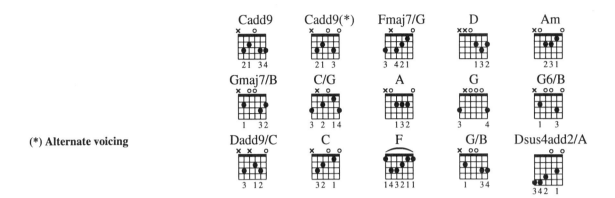

(*) Alternate voicing

Verse
Easy, relaxed

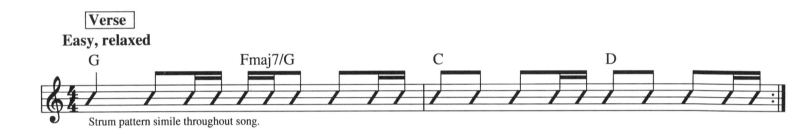

Strum pattern simile throughout song.

Solo

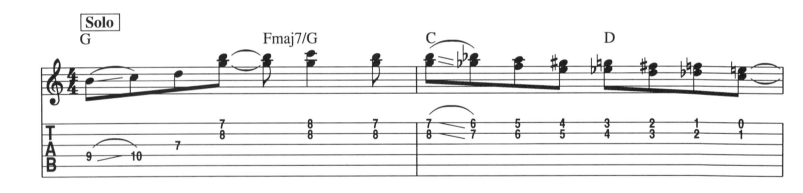

jonas & ezekial
(Guitar Parts)

Words and Music by
AMY RAY

* Capo 2nd Fret

Verse Strum Pattern

Repeat throughout verse.
* Song sounds one whole step higher than written.

Chorus Strum Pattern

End Of Chorus Fill

Capoed fret is represented by "0" in TAB.

Solo

Let It Be Me
(Guitar Parts)

Words and Music by
EMILY SALIERS

* Capo 3rd Fret

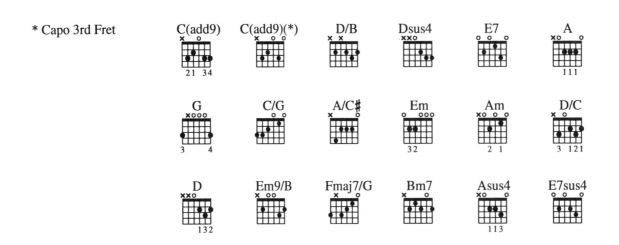

Intro
Easy, relaxed feel

* Song sounds a minor 3rd higher than written. Capoed fret is represented by "0" in TAB.

love will come to you
(Guitar Parts)

Words and Music by
EMILY SALIERS

virginia woolf
(Guitar Parts)

Words and Music by
EMILY SALIERS

Tuning: ⑥ D ③ G
⑤ A ② B
④ D ① C

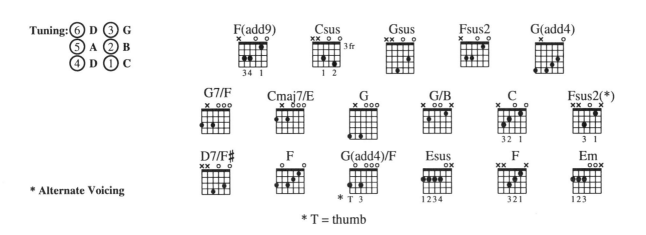

* Alternate Voicing

* T = thumb

Verse
Strictly

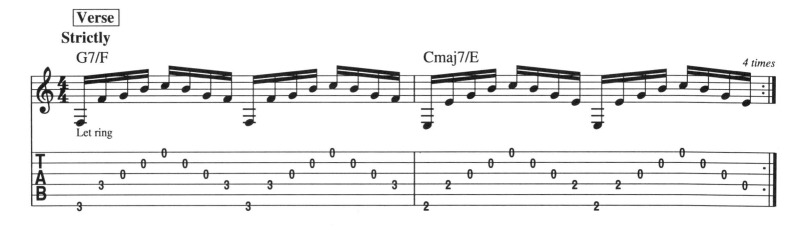

Interlude
Quickly

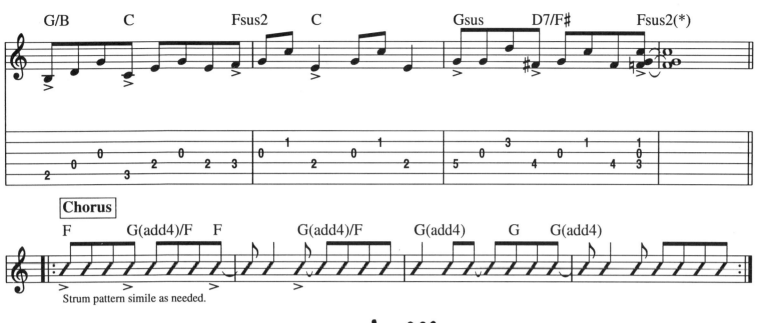

nashville
(Guitar Parts)

Words and Music by
AMY RAY

* Capo 2nd Fret

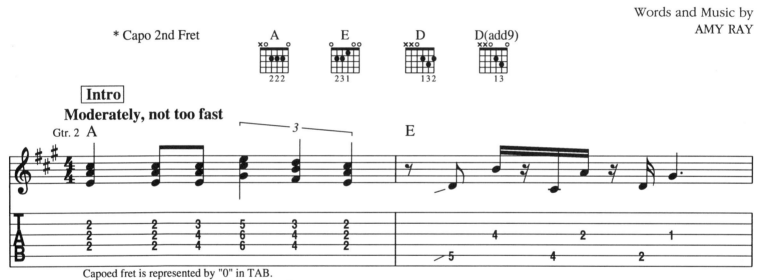

Capoed fret is represented by "0" in TAB.
* Song sounds one whole step higher than written.

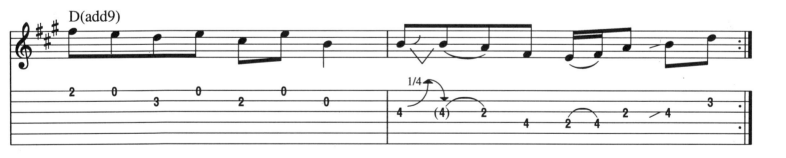

* Strum pattern simile throughout tune.

three hits
(Guitar Parts)

Words and Music by
AMY RAY

1st Verse

Moderately, not too fast

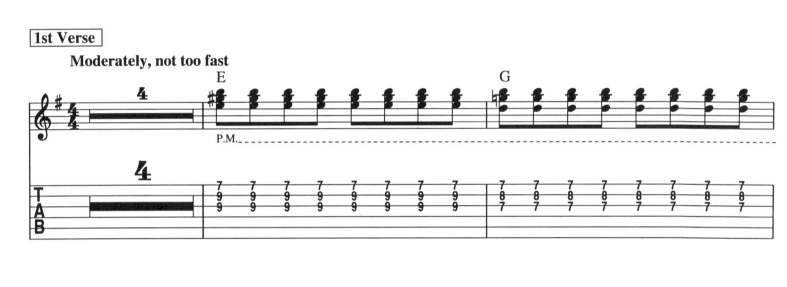

1st Bridge

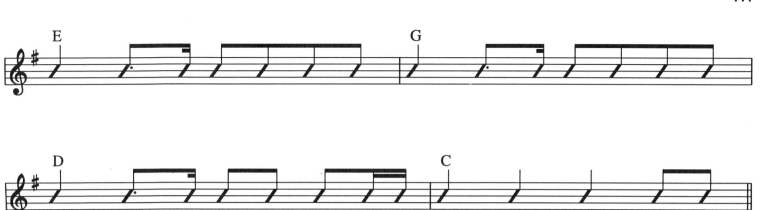

Acoustic Guitar Solo 1

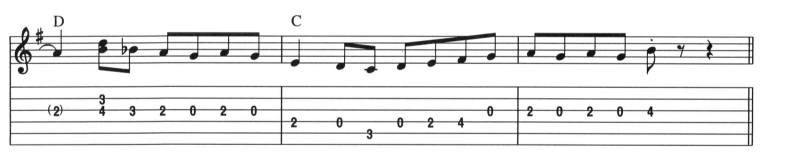

Pre-Solo Riff

Acoustic Guitar Solo 2

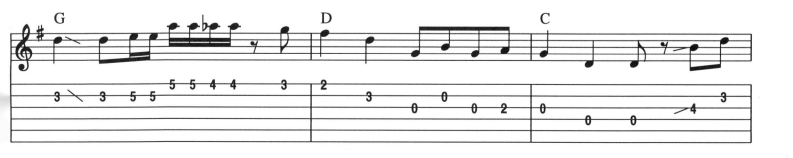

*3rd Verse

Let ring throughout

* Notes are derived from chord forms.

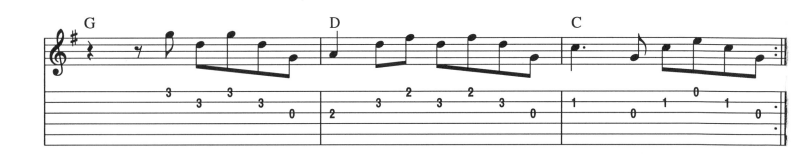

3rd Bridge

Ending Riff

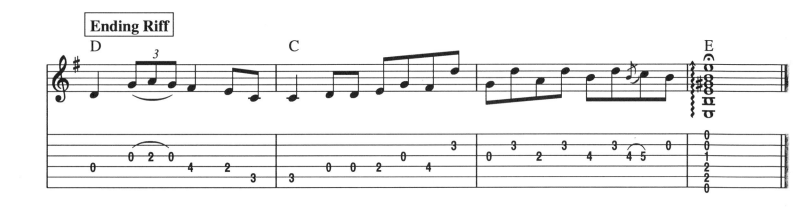